Sarmatians and Scythians

A Captivating Guide to the Barbarians of Iranian Origins and How These Ancient Tribes Fought Against the Roman Empire, Goths, Huns, and Persians

© **Copyright 2019**

All Rights Reserved. No part of this book may be reproduced in any form without permission in writing from the author. Reviewers may quote brief passages in reviews.

Disclaimer: No part of this publication may be reproduced or transmitted in any form or by any means, mechanical or electronic, including photocopying or recording, or by any information storage and retrieval system, or transmitted by email without permission in writing from the publisher.

While all attempts have been made to verify the information provided in this publication, neither the author nor the publisher assumes any responsibility for errors, omissions or contrary interpretations of the subject matter herein.

This book is for entertainment purposes only. The views expressed are those of the author alone, and should not be taken as expert instruction or commands. The reader is responsible for his or her own actions.

Adherence to all applicable laws and regulations, including international, federal, state and local laws governing professional licensing, business practices, advertising and all other aspects of doing business in the US, Canada, UK or any other jurisdiction is the sole responsibility of the purchaser or reader.

Neither the author nor the publisher assumes any responsibility or liability whatsoever on behalf of the purchaser or reader of these materials. Any perceived slight of any individual or organization is purely unintentional.

Free Bonus from Captivating History (Available for a Limited time)

Hi History Lovers!

Now you have a chance to join our exclusive history list so you can get your first history ebook for free as well as discounts and a potential to get more history books for free! Simply visit the link below to join.

Captivatinghistory.com/ebook

Also, make sure to follow us on Facebook, Twitter and Youtube by searching for Captivating History.

Contents

INTRODUCTION 1
PART I: THE SCYTHIANS 3
CHAPTER 1 – ORIGINS OF THE SCYTHIANS 4
CHAPTER 2 – ART, CULTURE, AND RELIGION 7
CHAPTER 3 – ECONOMY AND SOCIETY 11
CHAPTER 4 – WARFARE AND CONQUEST 15
CHAPTER 5 – END OF THE SCYTHIANS 24
PART II: THE SARMATIANS 27
CHAPTER 6 – ORIGINS OF THE SARMATIANS 28
CHAPTER 7 – ART, CULTURE, AND RELIGION 32
CHAPTER 8 – ECONOMY AND SOCIETY 36
CHAPTER 9 – WARFARE AND CONQUEST 41
CHAPTER 10 – END OF THE SARMATIANS 49
CONCLUSION 53

Introduction

Masters of the horse, the Scythians and Sarmatians opened the Eurasian Steppe to nomadic civilizations like it had never seen before. Following in the footsteps of the Cimmerians, a group of tribes sharing a common culture called the Steppe their home, adapting themselves to its harshness. Born out of this environment, a very particular way to live was adopted and later spread to peoples of Central Asia—the pastoral nomadic lifestyle. It would be the bane of organized armies of great empires, as the excellent mobility granted by their superior horse-riding skills were more than a match for the slow infantry that formed the backbone of the sedentary civilizations' armies.

The tale of the Scythians and Sarmatians have lasted through history, and although they had not one written historical record of their own, their presence was registered by dozens of classical historians. More importantly, though, their precious burial tombs still retained some of the civilizational remains of this extraordinary group of peoples.

The Scythians and Sarmatians had been deeply connected since their origin. The first Sarmatian people, the Sauromatae, were a part of the greater Scythian cultural group and spoke a dialect of the Scythian language. When the great Persian army invaded the Scythian territory in 513 BCE, the Sauromatae were listed among the allies of the Scythians, so we know they had friendly relations to some degree. However, later Sarmatian tribes wouldn't be so kind to the Scythians, and they eventually integrated part of them by subjugation. However, they both shared a fairly similar culture, and aside from the same language, they shared a common religious structure and practices, similar tribal organization, and similar clothing.

The Indo-European peoples commonly called as Scythians spanned the territory ranging from modern-day Romania to modern-day China. However, the Scythians and the Sarmatians mainly occupied the northern coast of the Black Sea, from modern-day Romania to the Volga River in modern-day southern Russia. The Scythians existed between, at least, the mid-8th century BCE and the 3rd century CE, while the Sarmatians (if we count the Sauromatae) existed between the 5th century BCE and the 5th century CE.

So, to tell the history of the Scythians and Sarmatians is to try to piece together a puzzle with a considerable amount of missing pieces, and it becomes even harder when one takes into account that some of the existing pieces have raised doubt about their veracity, as is the case with Herodotus, a Greek historian who lived around 484 to 425 BCE, who tells us about the Scythians in his *Histories*.

The goal of this book is then to gather and sort through the sources and present a concise but informative and accurate account of the history and legacy of the Scythians and Sarmatians.

Part I: The Scythians

Chapter 1 – Origins of the Scythians

The evidence for the existence of wagon nomadism, that is nomadic peoples that developed and used wagons for transportation of their belongings over large-distance migrations or nomadic behavior, can be traced as far back as the Bronze Age, but it is in the first millennium BCE that the archaeological data points to an increase of nomadic horse breeders in the northern Pontic region. It is only from the 8th century BCE onward that we start to know the name of the peoples who inhabited there, the Cimmerians and the Scythians, through the historical data. It is thought that the Scythians originated through the wave migrations of several ancient, related populations of the Indo-Iranian language group that came from Central Asia/southern Siberia.[1]

Geographically the full extent of the presence of the Scythians is not entirely known. However, it's known that they occupied a region ranging from the river Danube in the west to the river Don in the east and to the Black Sea in the south. This region was the core of their

---

[1] Bonfante, Larrisa – *The Barbarians of Ancient Europe: Realities and Interactions*. New York: Cambridge University Press, 2011. p. 110

civilization. Nevertheless, at certain times of expansion, this border could go farther and include the Caucasus and the Dobruja regions, to the southeast and west, respectively.[2]

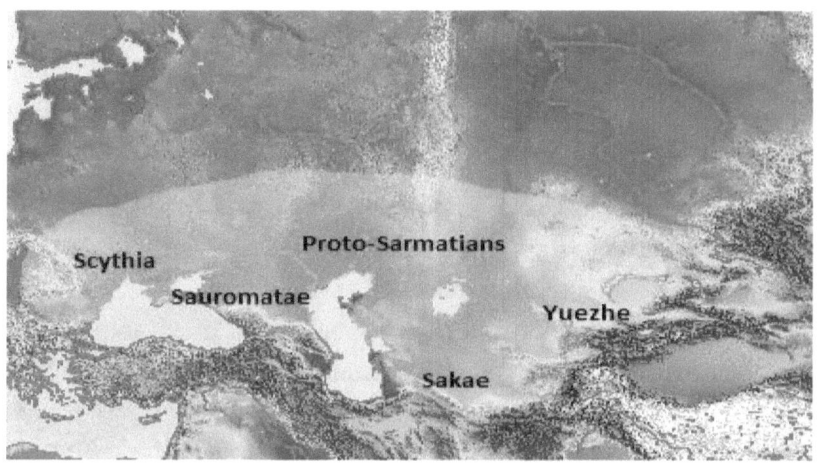

Figure 1 – Estimated maximum extent of the Indo-Iranian peoples, 500 BCE. Although they have different names, culturally they are all very similar to the point that they are all regarded as Scythian peoples.

It is thought that the geographical area occupied by the Scythians had an abundance of fertile soil and rivers, which provided optimal pasture lands for the Scythian nomadic horse-breeding civilization. However, reconstructing the landscape of the Scythians' home still remains a problem to solve among archaeologists.[3]

Their introduction in the historical records starts out with warfare, as their raids into the Near East's civilizations are registered in both cuneiform documents of Assyro-Babylonian origin and in the works of some authors of classical antiquity. Evidence of Scythian invasions is not only confirmed by the historical records but with archaeological findings of arrowheads, horse gear, and other items of Scythian origin as well. Archaeological data of the destruction of Urartian towns and fortresses also corroborate the Scythian

---

[2] Bonfante, Larrisa – *The Barbarians of Ancient Europe...* p. 109
[3] Bonfante, Larrisa – *The Barbarians of Ancient Europe...* p. 109

incursions into the Near East and the importance they played as a political destabilizer in the region.[4]

The Caucasus region was their entrance into the Near East, and their presence on the local tribes there is evident by the archaeological data. Scythian burial sites (*kurgans*) of a tribal chief and their mounted bodyguard were found in this region, and Scythian items are a frequent find in archaeological sites of local tribes.[5]

From this point onward, the Scythian peoples would influence the politics of the Near East and the Black Sea as they kept raiding their lands. However, during this process, the Scythians would also assimilate into their own culture the aspects they liked about other civilizations they contacted. Scythian material culture was enriched by their connection with the wealthy sedentary civilizations in both their complexity and material value. The luxury of the Near Eastern sedentary civilizations was captivating to the nomadic steppe tribes, and so, a process of cultural absorption started.[6]

---

[4] Bonfante, Larrisa – *The Barbarians of Ancient Europe...* p. 111. SINOR, Denis – *The Cambridge History of Early Inner Asia.* New York: Cambridge University Press, 1990. p. 99 & 100.
[5] Sinor, Denis – *The Cambridge History of Early Inner Asia.* New York: Cambridge University Press, 1990. p. 100.
[6] Sinor, Denis – *The Cambridge History of Early Inner Asia.* New York: Cambridge University Press, 1990. p. 100 & 101.

Chapter 2 – Art, Culture, and Religion

The Scythians had a language system of Indo-Iranian origin that influenced other nomadic Indo-Iranian peoples, like the Sarmatians, to an extent. Since they did not have any written records, any study on their language relies heavily on the Scythian words classical authors wrote down in their books, so it's very difficult to reconstruct how exactly they would have spoken.

Since we can't rely on original sources by the Scythians, some of our knowledge of their culture and religion is based on the artifacts found in archaeological sites. For instance, Scythian art reflected much of what their way of life looked like with a focus on the representation of animals (stags, birds, bears, etc.) with an emphasis on horses. This art was not only on physical objects but also on their own bodies, as they would tattoo these natural and animal iconographies. The early period of Scythian history featured Near Eastern, especially Assyro-Babylonian, influences on their artistic output as they came into contact with them via military incursions and raids. However, from the sixth century BCE onward, the Greek cultural influence can already be seen in their material culture, reaching an apex in the fourth century BCE.[7]

The absorption of Greek culture promoted by trade, especially in the fourth century BCE, reflected in the art style of their pieces. Gold ornaments, jewelry, hair combs, jugs, and other items began to feature a more pictorial and scenic style with decors of Scythian daily life or metaphysical events.[8]

The Scythian cultural enrichment during this phase wasn't synonymous with the enrichment of every individual but only of the chiefs or aristocracy who would be benefited by the cultural exchange that the Scythians had with other civilizations, at least in a "perpetual" sense, as the precious items of art would accompany the aristocratic Scythians in the afterlife.[9]

As commerce enriched them and the Greek cultural influence increased amongst the Scythian tribes, the nomadic or semi-nomadic tribes became more sedentary and settled in the northern Black Sea area, near Greek towns. A gradual change of the traditional burial method, with the *kurgans*, can also be seen during the fifth and fourth centuries. The conventional process of laying the body in a grave was done on a mattress or a primitive couch made of plant fibers; however, following Greek influence, the practice of using sarcophagi became more and more common, especially for the aristocratic members of society. In zones where the Greeks had direct contact with the Scythians, for example, Crimea, the royal and noble burials of the fifth and fourth centuries had the body laid in a sarcophagus.[10]

The Scythian religion was heavily influenced by the Indo-Iranian gods, and at the center of their pantheon was the goddess Tabiti who, according to Herodotus, was responsible for a safe and well-

---

[7] Jacobson, Esther – *The Art of the Scythians: The Interpenetration of cultures at the edge of the Hellenic world.* Leiden: E.J. Brill, 1995. Ch. 3. SINOR, Denis – *The Cambridge History of Early Inner Asia.* New York: Cambridge University Press, 1990. p. 109.
[8] Jacobson, Esther – *The Art of the Scythians...* Ch. 3.
[9] Sinor, Denis – *The Cambridge History of Early...* p. 109.

functioning household. The priest class, the Enarei, were thought by the Scythians to have the gift of prophecy, given to them by the goddess Argimpasa, queen of the heavens and mistress of the animals. To tell the future, the Enarei would use strips cut from the bark of the linden tree.

The Enarei also had the power to heal the Scythian king by divination, at least in Herodotus' narrative. To cure the king, the Enarei supposedly would find any men who had falsely sworn loyalty to the king, treating this treason as the cause of his disease, and then they would kill them. With the traitors punished for their treason, the king's health would, apparently, improve. [11] This passage by Herodotus tells us more than how the Enarei supposedly cured the king; it also gives us a clear idea of how much influence these priests held in Scythian society. By crossing the archaeological data with these narratives, we can confirm that religion indeed played a significant role in everyday life, and the Enarei had a critical role in it, so much so that they were buried with riches and precious ceremonial artifacts.

Herodotus also remarks that the Enarei dressed in the clothes of women and were hermaphrodites, as they were cursed by the goddess Aphrodite. In his *Histories*, Herodotus talks about this curse as a way to explain the "unusual Scythian femininity":

> So these Scythians who had plundered the temple at Ascalon, and their descendants forever, were smitten by the divinity with a disease which made them women instead of men: and the Scythians say that it was for this reason that they were diseased, and that for this reason travellers who visit Scythia now, see among them the affection of those who by the Scythians are called ENAREI.[12]

Although this curse is a myth, the fact that the Scythians believed it was true could have impacted the importance their society placed on

---

[10] Bonfante, Larrisa – *The Barbarians of Ancient Europe...* p. 85
[11] Herodotus – *Histories*. Book 4.68

women and that venerating them would please the gods and, thus, protect them from further punishment. However, the likely explanation of why the Scythians had a matriarchal society lies at the cultural heart of the Indo-Iranian primordial tribe from whom they originated. That culture probably had a social structure where women not only had a prominent place of power but more importantly, they had a deep connection with the divine forces. This is why both Scythian and Sarmatian tribes share this societal feature.

The Enarei were responsible for religious rituals as well, and besides animal sacrifices, which would include various types of livestock and in important occasions horses, the Scythians also used hemp and alcohol in these rituals to get into a spiritual trance.[13] Another religious ritual that the Sarmatians would also come to share with the Scythians was the practice of worshiping a god of war, who Herodotus equates to the Greek god Ares, by placing offerings onto small mounds made of brushwood where an iron sword was placed. The Scythians, in fact, unlike the Sarmatians, had a proper temple or earth mound, which was specifically dedicated to this kind of worship, meaning their place of worship would be semi-stationary and would be placed in locations reserved for these types of rituals.

---

[12] Herodotus – *Histories*. Book 1.105.
[13] Herodotus – *Histories*. Book 4.

Chapter 3 – Economy and Society

Scythians in the seventh century BCE lived in a communal tribal organization where social disparities between individuals wouldn't be very noticeable. However, as time went on and the Scythians secured more and more land and wealth, the accumulation of riches started to occur, primarily amongst the individuals with higher social standing who essentially became the aristocracy of said tribe. According to Herodotus, there were different types of Scythians, such as the Gargarii of the south of Ukraine (the Agricultural Scythians) and the so-called Royal Scythians who predominantly kept in the Crimean region. We don't know exactly how many individual tribes part of the Scythian cultural group were, but we do know that they weren't politically homogeneous and that they were made of smaller tribal groups who at some points would answer to a high-king who everyone would recognize either by their own volition or by subjugation. Some historians now theorize that the Gargarii weren't Scythians at all but were instead a kind of serf under Scythian domination and thus had to work for them. This reasoning justifies why they were sedentary and focused primarily on agricultural, something the Scythian nomads weren't very fond of. The Royal Scythians were named that way by Herodotus because most of the high-kings of the Scythian confederation came from this tribe, and this tells us that the Royal Scythians maintained a dominant position over the other tribes during an extended period.

It's still unclear if there were periods where there weren't any Scythian high-kings or if the high-king wasn't recognized as such by all of the tribal chieftains. Usually, a high-king from a dominant tribe would rule smaller tribal chieftains, who would then answer to him in a bond, similar to vassalage. This royal power was hereditary, and subject Scythian tribes would pay tribute and provide servants to the ruling tribe. Slaves were part of the Scythian society, but the evidence points to them being only domestic slaves and not used for other societal purposes.[14]

Furthermore, there is evidence that women would have had more significant participation in Scythian society than their Greek counterparts, occupying important societal roles and also fighting alongside men on the battlefield, thus being revered as great warriors. This is a feature shared by the other Indo-Iranian peoples like the Sarmatians, and at least in the Scythians' case, it would influence their pantheon of gods, in which goddesses like Argimpasa would have held a pivotal role in their beliefs. Scholars are not entirely sure if the Enarei priesthood would be held specifically by women or only by hermaphrodites, but either way, the Scythians venerated feminine characteristics. This can be seen in Scythian gold art where they depict humanoids who tend to be feminine.[15]

Scythian clothing was unisex, and both men and women wore kurtas, trousers, high boots or leather shoes, and a tunic with a round neck and long side openings, designed for horse riding. The kurtas, a loose collarless shirt, would have been made of woolen cloth, hemp, deerskin, or thick felt. Both commoners and aristocrats wore the same type of clothing, but the materials were different. As the Scythian civilization started to become richer, the aristocrats used

---

[14] Sinor, Denis – *The Cambridge History of Early...*. p. 104
[15] Bonfante, Larrisa – *The Barbarians of Ancient Europe...* p. 120

important materials for their clothing like silk or linen, oftentimes decorated with gold.[16]

The gold and precious loot accumulated by raids and pillages would have reaped great rewards for the Scythian aristocracy, a much more lucrative and significant economic activity would come to them from the Aegean Sea, particularly in the fourth century BCE. The Greek city-states required greats amounts of cereal crops, particularly during the Peloponnesian War, and would import them from the Scythians of the Bosporus. The Scythian aristocracy willing to accumulate Greek wealth would act as a mediator between the tribes of the East European forest-steppe, a perfect area for agriculture, and the Greeks. The aristocracy reaped excellent rewards from this "exploitation" of the agricultural Scythian communities, and this economic situation would be one of the forces behind the sedentarization of both the agrarian tribes and of the enriching aristocracy as well as one of the causes of the social gradation of wealth inequality between the common Scythian and the aristocracy.[17]

Aside from the exploitation of the agricultural Scythians, the Royal Scythians would also trade the products of their hunts and their animal husbandry, including pelts, furs, and other animal parts that were highly sought after by Mediterranean traders. Livestock and horses could have been something that they possibly traded with the Greek colonies of the Black Sea since the Scythians were predominantly animal breeders. With the result of their commerce, the Scythians would be able to buy precious manufactured materials such as jewelry, weapons, armor, and vases.

As a semi-nomadic group of tribes, the Scythians didn't have a centralized currency or financial system. Evidence of Scythian coin production has been found, and Strabo tells us of King Scilurus (who

---

[16] Encyclopedia Iranica – *Clothing of the Iranian Tribes on the Pontic Steppes and in the Caucasus* [Online] [Read 21/06/2019] Available at: http://www.iranicaonline.org/articles/clothing-vii

ruled in the latter half of the second century BCE) minting coins in the city of Olbia. These coins would come in two forms, either the primitive dolphin-shaped or arrowhead currency used for trading before the fifth century BCE or the imitations of Greek coins or Roman denarius, the Roman standard silver coin. They would also use Roman, Greek, or Pontic coins which they obtained through conquest or mercenary duties.

Scythian society was constructed around warfare, and the types of rituals they had and the items they carried to their grave show that being a victorious warrior had an impact on the social standing of an individual. Powerful commanders would take many precious items and artifacts to their graves, some acquired in faraway lands, and the most prestigious of the noblemen would even be buried with some of their warriors, servants, and horses.

---

[17] Sinor, Denis – *The Cambridge History of Early*…. p. 105

Chapter 4 – Warfare and Conquest

The start of the known Scythian conquests comes in the form of their incursions into the Caucasus and Near East, which was already discussed in the first chapter of this book. However, perhaps the most significant military achievement of early Scythian history is the epic tale of how they managed to defeat the military incursion of the mighty Persian king, Darius I, into Scythia around 513 BCE. King Darius I, alongside his great army (700,000 according to Herodotus, but in reality, it would have been substantially less), tried to subdue the Scythian tribes and thus stabilize his empire's border region with Scythia. He was met with a tribe of fast horse warriors that used guerilla tactics to weaken his army, avoiding open confrontation. They also applied scorched earth tactics, destroying and burning everything as they evaded Darius' army, making it so that Darius I couldn't live off their lands. This lasted the whole campaign, and the two forces would not engage each other in direct confrontation, at least as far as we know. However, Darius' efforts would be somewhat effective as they managed to subdue the subject peoples of the Scythians, such as the Budini, along the Black Sea coast. And while the scorched earth tactics may have been effective in helping to end the Persian attack, according to Herodotus, the Scythians ended up destroying most of their better lands. At the end of the Persian incursion, the Persians effectively controlled the major ports of the Black Sea, such as the city of Olbia, although this came at the cost of many Persian lives by the lack of supplies and the tactics of attrition on the part of the Scythians. The end of this military debacle would also bring about "written silence," since the Scythians would not be mentioned again in the classical sources until the campaigns of Philip II of Macedon in 329 BCE.[18]

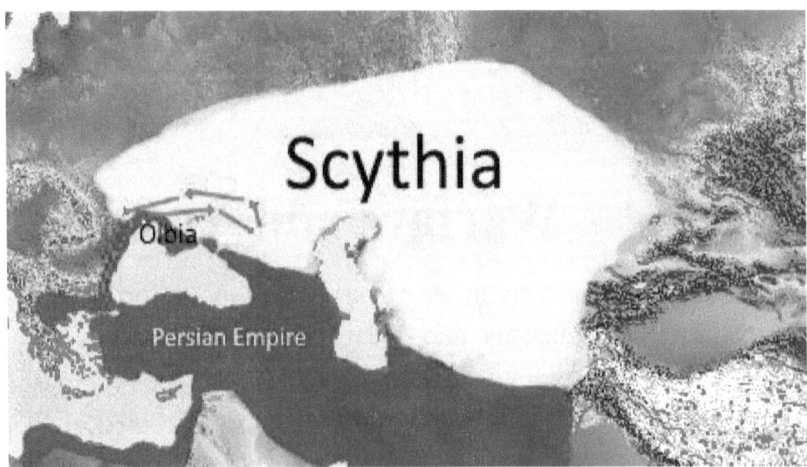

Figure 2 – Estimated path of Darius I's military incursion into Scythia, 513 BCE. The Scythian region represents the extension of the Indo-European tribes commonly referred to as Scythians because of their cultural similarity. Darius I's incursion was primarily against the European Scythians.

In 339 BCE, the Scythian king Ateas, a 90-year-old, became known for his military incursions into Thracia. He was successful at first and managed to conquer important areas from the Getae, a Thracian tribe that occupied the small area south of the Danube, as the fortified settlement of Eumolpia (modern-day Plovdiv, Bulgaria), but he was ultimately defeated and killed by the Macedonian king Philip II. The aftermath of Ateas' defeat was the capture of 20,000 women and 20,000 horses by the Macedonian king.[19]

Although this defeat weakened the Scythian hold on their western territories and the Getae managed to cross the Danube into their

---

[18] Sinor, Denis – *The Cambridge History of Early....* p. 101
[19] Sinor, Denis – *The Cambridge History of Early....* p. 106

lands, their civilization would still thrive until the latter half of the third century when their hold on the Eurasian Steppe was seriously challenged by the Sarmatians and the Celts. This effectively ended the Scythian domination in the Eurasian Steppe and pushed them into two smaller and sperate kingdoms, known as the Crimean Little Scythia and the Thracian Little Scythia, which will be explained in more detail in the next chapter.[20]

In 329 BCE, a young Macedonian general named Alexander conquered the whole Persian Empire, which was under the rule of Darius III. After this, he sought to solidify his conquests and expand into India. At the southern bank of the river Jaxartes (modern-day Syr Darya), Alexander had built a city to delimitate the border of his empire. The city was called Alexandria Eschate (located in modern-day Khujand, Tajikistan). The local population of Sogdians, an ancient Iranian civilization, did not like this intrusion into their land and revolted. The peoples that lived across the Jaxartes, the Scythians or Sacae, saw this revolt as a great opportunity to loot and pillage the Greeks, so they joined forces with the Sogdians. To end this instability on his northern borders, Alexander took the matter into his own hands and personally led the battle against the Scythians and Sogdians.

Since the Jaxartes was wider than a bow shot, the Greek troops should have been able to board their ships and rafts in safety. However, their crossing would be within the Scythian fire range, meaning they could potentially be hit by incoming arrows. To prevent this, a plan was devised: The Greek catapult would be placed right next to the shore where they would then have the range to hit the Scythian forces and continuously fire until the whole army had crossed safely. The plan worked, and in the first round of catapult fire, a Scythian leader was killed, alongside many other Scythians. The Greek archers were the first to cross so that they could protect the rest of the army by keeping the Scythian forces at a distance. After them followed the cavalry and finally the infantry. To force the

---

[20] Sinor, Denis – *The Cambridge History of Early*.... p. 107

Scythians into direct confrontation, Alexander sent his auxiliary light cavalry forces to bait the Scythians into an attack. This was successful, and the Scythians surrounded the auxiliary cavalry and engaged in close-quarters combat. Now the rest of Alexander's army had a chance to engage the Scythians and defeat them, which they did. The infantry and archers quickly surrounded the Scythian forces, catching those who sought to flee the onslaught and defeating the main Scythian army. The aftermath of this battle resulted in 1,200 Scythians killed and 1,800 horses captured.

The last detailed account of a Scythian battle in the written classical sources took place between 310 and 309 BCE when the Scythians intervened in the Bosporan Civil War, a dynastic dispute among the heirs of the Bosporan Kingdom. Satyrus II, the eldest heir, inherited the throne, but his brother Eumelos contested his claim. Fearing persecution from his older brother, Eumelos fled the capital and was offered refuge by the Siraces, a tribe of the Sarmatians, who seized the opportunity to gain influence in the Bosporus and try to take lands from the Scythians. The king of the Siraces, Aripharnes, and Eumelos allied with one another and gathered a force of 20,000 horsemen and 22,000 foot soldiers. Satyrus responded by mobilizing an army of 2,000 Greek troops and a similar number of Thracian mercenaries. However, the core of Satyrus' army was made up of 10,000 Scythian horsemen and 20,000 Scythian foot soldiers.

The Bosporan army (34,000) was at a disadvantage and was outnumbered by the Siraces (42,000). This situation was aggravated by the lack of forage for the Scythian horses, which had to be carried by wagon in a long and slow supply train. When they reached the Siracen army, they found the enemy on the northern bank of the river Thatis, ready to engage in battle in a more advantageous position. Satyrus made the bold move of crossing the river to attack them, using the wagon supply train to make a fortified camp which they could defend until the whole army had crossed. This move was surprisingly successful, and once all the forces were ready, he immediately drew them to the front of the makeshift fort. Ready to face the Siraces, Satyrus placed the Greek and Thracian troops in the right wing of his battle line, some of the Scythian cavalry and infantry in the left wing, and heavy Scythian cavalry in the center. We know little of the Siracen battle line, however. We can only assume that Eumelos and their cavalry were on the left flank, facing the Greek and Thracian mercenaries, with the infantry on the right wing. Aripharnes was at the center, also with heavy cavalry.

The battle was fierce, and both sides suffered heavy losses as soon as it began. Eumelos met with success against the Greek and Thracian mercenaries, causing them to waver, but, at the same time, Satyrus and the Scythians had managed to defeat Aripharnes' heavy cavalry. The Bosporan king, watching his left side collapse, quickly moved behind Eumelos' rear and charged in an all-out attack, smashing him between the Greeks and Scythians. Having been defeated, the surviving Siraces fled the battlefield and took refuge at a nearby fortress. The Scythian-Bosporan combined might was victorious.

This battle exemplifies the speed at which the Scythian forces could move and rearrange their positions to suit their needs. The might of their cavalry and the speed at which they conducted their attacks were difficult to counter in the ancient battlefield and was generally very effective against heavy infantry.

Scythian warfare was typically done on horseback, and thus, their army had a lot of cavalries. This gave them an advantage over traditional armies of the complex civilizations of the Near East that were overly dependent on infantry. Mounted archers were vital in the Scythian army as they gave them sufficient range to keep them free from engaging with the enemy but could also kill somewhat effectively. Their practice with the bow on horseback made them skilled shooters, but it was the fast-repeated volleys of arrows that did more significant damage. They would use guerrilla tactics to deceive their enemies while bombarding them with volley after volley of arrows and darts, and after the enemy broke their unit cohesion, the Scythians would charge in with lances and close-quarter weapons.[21] Herodotus stated that the Scythians "who have neither cities founded nor walls built, but carry their houses with them and are mounted archers, living not by the plow but by cattle, and whose dwellings are upon carts, these assuredly are invincible and impossible to approach."[22]

The most famous representation of Scythian armor is that of the scale armor, but early Scythian attempts at defensive wares were much simpler and consisted of animal leather or hide which, in some case, were covered by plates of iron or bronze. Only after their contact with Mesopotamian smiths and armorers would the Scythians develop the much more effective scale armor, which better protected the torso against spear or arrow penetration. Scale armor would prove so popular amongst the Scythian ranks that it remained the main armor of the Scythian armies until their disappearance in the fourth century CE.[23]

The helmet also naturally evolved as the Scythians came into contact with new types of warfare and new models made by other civilizations. Around the sixth century BCE, the Scythians used a cast-bronze helmet which gave good protection to the lower parts and the back of the head. This type of helmet is commonly named the "Kuban helmet," as it was found in archaeological excavations around the Kuban area (a region in modern-day southern Russia). However, from the fifth century BCE to the third century CE, along with their body armor, the Scythians would use a scale helmet. This piece of headgear constituted of a pointed leather cap which was then covered with overlapping metal scales. This scale type of construction, like the body armor, gave good protection against sword and spear attacks, and so, it was widely used among the Scythians. Alongside the adoption of the scale helmet, another

---

[21] Chernenko, E.V. – *The Scythians 700-300 BC*. Oxford: Osprey Publishing, 1983.
[22] Herodotus – *Histories*. Book 4. 46.
[23] Chernenko, E.V. – *The Scythians...* p. 7.

model would be adopted by the Scythian aristocracy—Greek helmets of either Corinthian, Chalcidian, or Attic origins.[24]

Scythian weaponry consisted of three types: long-range melee weapons (spears and lances), close-range melee weapons (daggers and swords), and mobile projectile weapons (javelins and bows). Spears would be used extensively by mounted or foot warriors to thrust their enemy at a safe distance and for throwing. They would be between 170 to 180 centimeters (5.5 to almost 6 feet) long. Evidence of longer spears and lances was found in some Scythian burial mounds, but it has such a rare occurrence that historians think that these types of weapons (that could reach up to three meters long) were only used by specialized cavalry units, due to requiring higher skill to maneuver them successfully.[25]

Swords and daggers were used by the Scythians, but it was more of an important tool for rituals and religious practices than combat. Some of the most impressive Scythian swords found to this day in archaeological excavations are merely ceremonial ones, made of gold and adorned with the Scythian animal art style. That is not to say that they didn't use the sword in combat; in fact, there is evidence that they used two types of swords, short and long ones, with the latter having more practical use in mounted combat due to its longer range.[26]

Other weapons used by mounted warriors include the javelin, which was basically a smaller spear that had a small, sharp pyramid head. While it was mainly used to disable shields or slightly injure the enemy, it still could kill or gravely injure someone.[27]

Lastly, the bow was, without a doubt, the most popular weapon used by the Scythians, and arrowheads were found in burial mounds of commoners and kings alike. It was the essential weapon for these warriors. The bow had a curved structure, and its length was up to

---

[24] Chernenko, E.V. – *The Scythians...* p. 7
[25] Chernenko, E.V. – *The Scythians...* p. 17
[26] Chernenko, E.V. – *The Scythians...* p. 14
[27] Chernenko, E.V. – *The Scythians...* p. 19

120 centimeters (a little less than 4 feet). The bow was mighty, but stiff and considerable strength would have been needed to master its use. Once mastered, the bow revealed to be a potent long-range projectile weapon that could shoot arrows up to a distance of 200 or more yards. The arrows were made of a reed or branch staff and a metal or bone tip, with the fletching made from birds' feathers.[28]

The people conquered by the Scythians would meet a ruthless and powerful foe, which, according to Herodotus, would not have mercy upon them and would practice human sacrifices. Historians cannot say for sure if the bloody practices Herodotus describes of their captives are true or if he is just portraying the Scythians as inhumane and barbarians to transmit the idea that the Greeks were culturally superior. Either way, the following excerpt of Herodotus' *Histories* remains a compelling read and can give us some idea of what the Scythian customs were:

> That which relates to war is thus ordered with them:—When a Scythian has slain his first man, he drinks some of his blood: and of all those whom he slays in the battle he bears the heads to the king; for if he has brought a head he shares in the spoil which they have taken, but otherwise not. And he takes off the skin of the head by cutting it round about the ears and then taking hold of the scalp and shaking it off; afterwards he scrapes off the flesh with the rib of an ox, and works the skin about with his hands; and when he has thus tempered it, he keeps it as a napkin to wipe the hands upon, and hangs it from the bridle of the horse on which he himself rides, and takes pride in it; for whosoever has the greatest number of skins to wipe the hands upon, he is judged to be the bravest man. Many also make cloaks to wear of the skins stripped off, sewing them together like shepherds' cloaks of skins; and many take the skin together with the finger-nails off the right hands of their enemies when they are dead, and

---

[28] Chernenko, E.V. – *The Scythians...* p. 11 & 12

make them into covers for their quivers: now human skin it seems is both thick and glossy in appearance, more brilliantly white than any other skin. Many also take the skins off the whole bodies of men and stretch them on pieces of wood and carry them about on their horses…(…)Once every year each ruler of a district mixes in his own district a bowl of wine, from which those of the Scythians drink by whom enemies have been slain; but those by whom this has not been done do not taste of the wine, but sit apart dishonoured; and this is the greatest of all disgraces among them: but those of them who have slain a very great number of men, drink with two cups together at the same time.[29]

---

[29] Herodotus – *Histories*. Book 4. 64-66

Chapter 5 – End of the Scythians

The tale of the end of the Scythians comes to us via the Greek philosopher and historian Strabo. According to him, from the second century BCE to the first century CE, two minor Scythian kingdoms resisted the onslaught from the Celts and Sarmatians. One of them was situated south of the Danube River and is thought to have been formed by the Scythians who remained after King Ateas' defeat after the other Scythians returned to the northern Black Sea coast. The other minor Scythian kingdom was located in what is known today as the peninsula of Crimea and went as far north as the region of Taurida (modern-day South Ukraine). Neapolis, the capital of the Crimean kingdom, was where the Scythian royal and aristocratic headquarters were based and from where the Scythian high-king would have ruled the Scythian confederation.[30]

The Crimean kingdom had significant cultural and economic development in the second century BCE. In a measure to centralize their Mediterranean trade and stop dealing with the Greek mediators, they successfully attacked the Greek towns of the northwest Chersonesus Taurica (the Greek Crimean colonies). Commanded by King Scilurus, the Scythians managed to conquer all of the

---

[30] Sinor, Denis – *The Cambridge History of Early…*. p. 107

northwestern Crimean Greek colonies, some being completely devastated and razed to the ground while others became occupied by the Scythians who built their fortresses on their ruins. The ones who didn't want to end in ruin submitted to Scythian domination, like the town of Olbia where King Scilurus made his coins.[31]

The effort made by Scilurus to expand their power and drive out the Greek commercial mediators was complemented by what the evidence points out as being the existence of a Scythian fleet, which would have allowed Scythian merchants to safely conduct trade of their agricultural goods directly with the Mediterranean.[32]

The death of Scilurus and the succession of his son Palacus would mark a turning point of the Scythian offensive toward the Greek colonies as the remaining ones would turn to the Pontic kingdom for help. Mithridates VI, also known as Mithridates the Great, the king of Pontus, answered the Greek call for help and sent an army commanded by the general Diophantus. The Pontic army delivered a bitter defeat to the Scythian and Sarmatian combined force, as Palacus had enlisted the Roxolani, a Sarmatian tribe, to help deal with the Pontic army, and managed to protect the Greek domains, although the Greeks wouldn't fully recuperate all the territories they had lost under the reign of Scilurus.[33]

The defeat at the hands of the Pontic army was brutal, but open hostilities would resume again later in the first century CE, at which point the Greek Chersonese sought help from the Romans. A Roman expedition was then mounted to liberate the Greeks from constant harassment that culminated in the year 63 CE with a Scythian defeat. Archaeological evidence ranging from the first to the second century CE point to the destruction of Scythian forts by the Roman military presence in the area.[34]

---

[31] Sinor, Denis – *The Cambridge History of Early...*. p. 108
[32] Sinor, Denis – *The Cambridge History of Early...*. p. 108
[33] Sinor, Denis – *The Cambridge History of Early...*. p. 108
[34] Sinor, Denis – *The Cambridge History of Early...*. p. 108

The Scythians, after all of these military failures, weren't totally driven off their lands, and evidence shows that they still persisted through the second and beginning of the third centuries CE. It is by the middle of the third century CE that we can no longer find evidence of a culturally distinct Scythian population. They were assimilated by the Goths and other nomadic peoples that passed through the Bosporus region, and they lost their cultural and linguistic cohesion, marking the de facto end of what we broadly call the Scythians.

Part II: The Sarmatians

Chapter 6 – Origins of the Sarmatians

The first reference to the term "Sauromatae" comes via the Greek writer Herodotus in his *Histories* to describe a nomadic people that lived south of the river Don and the Volga. He refers to them as being the sons of a Scythian father and an Amazon mother, which to him justified why they spoke a "broken-dialect" of the Scythian language. The basis of this affirmation is, of course, only mythical; however, by analyzing and cross-referencing the various classical authors and the archaeological data, academics have been able to conclude that both Scythian and Sauromatae tribes originated from the peoples of the Bronze Age Srubnaya culture, located on the northern shore of the Black Sea and covering a large part of the Pontic-Caspian steppe (modern-day southern Russia and Kazakhstan). Some of the tribes of the Srubnaya culture cooperated with tribes from the Andronovo culture, whose presence covered almost all of modern-day Kazakhstan, and were influenced by them culturally, which can explain why the Sauromatae spoke a "broken-dialect" of the Scythian language.[35]

---

[35] Sinor, Denis – *The Cambridge History of Early...*. p. 110

The Sauromatae, like the Scythians, were not a single unified entity but rather a group of different tribes that shared a common cultural background. They mostly stayed in the territory southeast of the river Don between the sixth and seventh century BCE, but starting at the end of the fifth century, the Sauromatae crossed the Don and established themselves in the coast of the Azov Sea.

The close proximity between the Sauromatae and the Scythians, both in geographic and cultural terms, transpired in peaceful cooperation between the two groups of peoples. So much so that when the Persian emperor Darius I sent a military incursion to end the Scythian menace, the Sauromatae were counted amongst the Scythian allies.[36]

Although the Sauromatae shared a genetic link with the later Sarmatians, they are not the same thing, and a direct line of development can't be established between the two peoples more clearly because the Sarmatians developed differently than the Sauromatae even though the two eventually crossed paths and intermixed with each other.[37]

The Proto-Sarmatian group of peoples originated in the area south of the Ural Mountains and ultimately, between the fourth and third centuries BCE, migrated to the region south of the Volga and southeast of the Don, conquering the Sauromatae that lived there. The mixing of these peoples, the Sarmatians, and the Sauromatae, is at the core of the origin of the Sarmatian tribes we later see mentioned in the sources of antiquity—the Aorsi, Siraces, Roxolani, Alans, and the Iazyges.[38]

---

[36] Brzezinski, R; Mielczarek, M – *The Sarmatians 600 BC–AD 450* Oxford: Osprey Publishing, 2002. p. 7
[37] Brzezinski, R; Mielczarek, M – *The Sarmatians*. p. 6 & 7; SINOR, Denis – *The Cambridge History of Early...*. p. 112
[38] Sinor, Denis – *The Cambridge History of Early...*. p. 112

Figure 3 – Estimated maximum extension of the Sarmatians and the main tribe's location in the 1st century CE. The Alans originated only in the 1st century CE and assimilated the Aorsi and probably the remaining Siraces.

The Siraces were Sarmatians that migrated to the Black Sea/Sea of Azov coast, south of the Don, in the late fifth century BCE. They often appear in classical works alongside the Bosporan Kingdom, who they maintained close relations with. At one point, Strabo mentions that the Siraces during the reign of King Abeacus were able to raise around 20,000 riders. From what we can conclude though, they were a relatively smaller tribe, so we can't confirm that this is accurate. The close proximity they maintained between the Pontic and Bosporan Kingdoms made them the most Hellenized of the Sarmatians, and although most of their aristocracy kept a semi-nomadic lifestyle, most of the population was sedentary.[39]

The Aorsi lived in the open plateau south of the Don and northeast of the Siraces. Strabo indicates that the Aorsi was one of the most prominent Sarmatian peoples and was, in fact, divided between the lower and upper Aorsi. The lower Aorsi was described as being able to field around 200,000 riders and lived in the plateau south of the Don. The upper Aorsi occupied a more significant area consisting of

---

[39] Brzezinski, R; Mielczarek, M – *The Sarmatians*. p. 7

all the cost of the Caspian Sea, and modern studies have traced their influence all the way to the Aral Sea.[40]

The Roxolani and Iazyges were in the vanguard of the Sarmatian move westward, and all evidence points to them as being the first Sarmatians to cross the river, Don. The two tribes were located in different geographical zones; the Roxolani mostly kept themselves in the region south of Ukraine of the forest-steppe, while the Iazyges kept to the Crimean territories and the coast of the Black Sea/Azov Sea. Their gradual advancement westward of the Don started in the second century BCE and lasted until the Roxolani had reached the region of Moesia in the first century CE and threatened the eastern region of the Roman Empire.[41]

The Alans were the last of what we call the Sarmatian tribes to appear in the Black Sea region coming from Central Asia in the mid-first century CE. They are described as not being wholly Sarmatian and are thought to have had a tribal composition of both Central Asian and Sarmatian origins. Some authors of antiquity point to the Sarmatian part of the Alans having originated in the tribe of the Massagetae, who had mixed with several Saka peoples and other Central Asians. [42]

---

[40] Brzezinski, R; Mielczarek, M – *The Sarmatians*. p. 7 & 8
[41] Brzezinski, R; Mielczarek, M – *The Sarmatians*. p. 8
[42] Brzezinski, R; Mielczarek, M – *The Sarmatians*. p. 10

Chapter 7 – Art, Culture, and Religion

The absence of Sarmatian written sources makes it somewhat difficult to pinpoint what exactly their culture and religion were like. From the archaeological data and the classical sources, we can infer some information about the way these people lived and their cultural traditions.

Some historians have the opinion that the cultural output of the Sarmatians was less developed than the Scythians, meaning that the archaeological materials that have been found are often less complex in detail and less rich. The frequency of the richer artifacts is also less than the Scythians.[43]

Nevertheless, the Sarmatian artifacts are still impressive in their own right and are the physical proof of their artistical achievements. Today, we can find some of them in the Sarmatian collection of the State Hermitage Museum in St. Petersburg, Russia, that boast an extensive and magnificent collection of precious artifacts. There are multiple kinds of gold Sarmatian artifacts, including golden torques, perfume flasks, and diadems; these all share the same art style—the so-called polychrome Sarmatian animal style. Notable for the

---

[43] Sinor, Denis – *The Cambridge History of Early...*. p. 111

representation of the heads and bodies of animals in their ornaments, the polychrome Sarmatian style was the result of the deep connection the Sarmatians had with nature and the importance it had to them.[44]

The few Sarmatian art pieces that made their way to us are here thanks to the burial rituals which, similar to the Scythians, constituted of underground structures beneath an earthen mound where they buried their dead in rectangular rooms and included personal items, gifts, and offerings. In the burial mounds of the important Sarmatian individuals, various gold items, like bracelets, torques, or even belt buckles, have been found, displaying their wealth. If the individual was female, then precious jewelry pieces like rings or necklaces made of gold accompanied the dead.[45]

The Sarmatian animal art style is also indicative of their religious veneration with nature and their use of animal and ritualistic sacrifices. Although not much is known about their specific gods or goddesses, we know some tidbits of information. We know that through historical evidence from the Alan tribe that the Sarmatians probably worshiped a pantheon of seven gods—the norm amongst tribes of Indo-Iranian origins. Amongst their pantheon, historians are almost certain that the Sarmatians worshiped a god of water and fire, which was also very common amongst Indo-Iranian tribes. One particular religious practice that we know of through the records of the Roman Ammianus Marcellinus is the worship of a god, similar to the Roman god Mars; this ritual was consummated by driving a sword into a small earth mound. In a representation of the erection of the "axis mundi" (in ancient religions, the axis mundi represented the "umbilical cord" that unites the world of gods with the world of humans, and erecting an axis mundi meant to create a site where this

---

[44] The State Hermitage Museum. *Treasures from the Sarmatians*. HermitageMuseum.org. 24 May 2019
< https://www.hermitagemuseum.org>
[45] The State Hermitage Museum. *Treasures from the Sarmatians*. HermitageMuseum.org. 24 May 2019
< https://www.hermitagemuseum.org>

"umbilical cord" could exist), the ritual likely symbolized the connection of the people with their gods, a practice that the Sarmatians shared with their Scythian cousins, who, unlike them, had specially dedicated altars for this specific ritual. Outside of these altars, we don't have any archaeological data of Sarmatian buildings that were used specifically as temples, which suggests they didn't have any.[46]

Sarmatian burials and religion were interconnected since the burial of a deceased individual was done according to their religious beliefs. Aside from preparing a journey to some kind of afterlife, evidence of their worship of fire can be found in their burial mounds. Remnants of a ritual bonfire, which was used to cover the graves, have been found, as well as a ring made of its ash inside the grave. The prevalent role of fire with Sarmatian graves is not fully understood, but it gives us a clear indication that to these people fire was essential for the burial ritual. The close proximity of the burial mounds suggests that the Sarmatians practiced some type of ancestor veneration and that Sarmatians liked to be buried close to their ancestors. Of course, this doesn't necessarily mean that ancestor veneration was an essential part of their religious customs but was rather a cultural practice that was of vital importance to these peoples.[47]

In burial mounds of some Sarmatian women, what would be considered a small portable altar— a small stone plate—that was used for various ritual activities, such as igniting ritual fires or grinding chalk, has been found. The fact that these portable altars have only been found, so far, in burial mounds of women indicates that only women could be priestesses or, at the very least, that they were the only ones that could use them religiously.[48]

---

[46] Encyclopedia of Religion. *Sarmatian Religion*. Encyclopedia.com. 3 Jun. 2019<https://www.encyclopedia.com>.
[47] Encyclopedia of Religion. *Sarmatian Religion*. Encyclopedia.com. 3 Jun. 2019<https://www.encyclopedia.com>.
[48] Encyclopedia of Religion. *Sarmatian Religion*. Encyclopedia.com. 3 Jun. 2019<https://www.encyclopedia.com>.

The Sarmatians practiced cultural body deformation, and although we are not totally sure if the accounts by the Roman geographer Pomponius Mela (15–45 CE) of breast cauterization in women are true, we do have archaeological evidence that the Alans practiced head elongation. In their infancy, Alan children could be bandaged in the head so that they would have an elongated cranial structure when they were older. The purpose of this practice, outside a culture sense of "fashion," is not very well understood, but the frequency of elongated skulls in the archaeological data dated between the second and fourth centuries CE points to this practice being popularized by Hunnic influences.[49]

Body tattoos were also a common practice among Sarmatian peoples, and, according to the Roman philosopher and historian Sextus Empiricus (160–210 CE), they were tattooed in their infancy. The tattoos would have been likely made in the Sarmatian animal style, given the importance it had to the Sarmatians culturally.

All of what we know of the art, culture, and religion of the Sarmatians corroborate the narrative that historically the Scythians and the Sarmatians had very close cultural ties, not only in linguistic terms but also in cultural practices.

---

[49] Brzezinski, R; Mielczarek, M – *The Sarmatians*. p. 13

Chapter 8 – Economy and Society

Economically, the Sarmatians weren't too different from the Scythians. As a semi-nomadic group of tribes, these peoples would depend on agriculture and animal husbandry to not only sustain themselves but to also trade with other civilizations. Hunting played a large part in their economy since the furs and pelts they gathered would garner a high price in the Mediterranean and Pontic areas. Some of their material wealth and precious artifacts would come from raiding and warfare, as their high mobility would give them the capability of gathering quick pillaging parties to gain loot from neighboring settlements. This form of warfare was the result of their mastery of horse riding and their reliance on the horse for their martial activities, which made them have a cavalry that was much larger than other civilizations at this time.[50]

Another point to consider in terms of their economic structure and something that can't be disregarded was their work as mercenaries on the payroll of wealthy empires or kingdoms, such as the Bosporan Kingdom and the Roman Empire. Not only would they be paid handsomely for their services, but their loyalty and good behavior

---

[50] Sinor, Denis – *The Cambridge History of Early...*. p. 115

would be rewarded with precious gifts made of gold or other valuable materials.[51]

The upper Aorsi, and later the Alans, had access to other types of riches since the important trade routes that came to the Black Sea from Mesopotamia and India gave them a type of material wealth that other Sarmatian tribes couldn't manage to achieve. Strabo describes this well in his passage:

> But the upper Aorsi sent a still larger number, for they held dominion over more land, and, one may almost say, ruled over most of the Caspian coast; and consequently, they could import on camels the Indian and Babylonian merchandise, receiving it in their turn from the Armenians and the Medes, and also, owing to their wealth, could wear golden ornaments.[52]

The Sarmatians had no official coinage or complex financial system. Instead, they would trade either by bartering or using coins from other civilizations, such as Roman and Greek coins. In the Black Sea region, cities from other kingdoms like the Greek Olbia and Bosporan Chersonesus would be responsible for coin mintage, and when these types of towns would be conquered by the Sarmatians or the Scythians, they would use it to strike their own coins, which imitated Greek ones.[53]

The Sarmatians were a tribal society and shared many features with other similar contemporary civilizations, primarily the Scythians. The Sarmatians were divided amongst many tribes that together had a familiar culture and language, but each tribe was independent and had a "king" or "chief" figure. On certain occasions, these leaders would unite to rule over great confederations of peoples, as was the case with the Alans, Roxolani, Iazyges, Aorsi, and Siraces. All of

---

[51] Brzezinski, R; Mielczarek, M – *The Sarmatians*. p. 15
[52] Strabo – *Geography*. Book 6. 8 [Online] [Read 26/05/2019] Available at: http://penelope.uchicago.edu/Thayer/E/Roman/Texts/Strabo/11E*.html

these tribes were confederations and were formed either by the subjugation of many smaller tribes or by tribal initiative, meaning that the tribes would have come together by their own volition and then elect a king from a tribe that everyone respected. We are not entirely sure why they created confederations due to a tribal initiative; presumably, it was to become stronger as a cultural group or to seek the opportunities a tribe could have in such confederations, such as ease of access to better loot. It is thought that all the Sarmatian confederations mentioned above were created by free tribal aggregation, but they all, at some point or another, integrated smaller tribes forcefully.

This was not the only thing that the Sarmatians shared in common with the Scythians, as they also wore similar clothing. Both men and women would wear short cloaks, caftans (a traditional type of shirt) that opened in the front, loose trousers, and headdresses with one or two disks over the forehead. They wore high boots, leather stockings, shoes with a pointy front, or high felt boots. Women could also be seen wearing a sleeveless dress fastened at each shoulder with a fibula. To this day, caftans are still worn in the regions the Sarmatians influenced. The difference between aristocratic and commoner clothing was the materials from which the wares were made. Sarmatian aristocrats wore clothing made from silk and linen that was decorated with gold ornaments; all of these were imported materials from the Mediterranean civilizations.[54] Sarmatians would primarily trade natural goods for manufactured ones from their Mediterranean trading partners. From Greek clothing and helmets to jewelry, the Sarmatians would seek these goods, and in exchange, they would sell or barter pelts, furs, domestic animal products, and agricultural goods.

---

[53] Grumeza, Lavinia – *Roman Coins in Sarmatian Graves from the Territory of Banat (2nd-4th centuries AD)*. Analele Banatului Arcaheologie-Istorie. Cluj-Napoca: Editura MEGA. ISSN 1221-678X. N° 21 (2013). p. 117-128.
[54] Encyclopedia Iranica – *Clothing of the Iranian Tribes on the Pontic Steppes and in the Caucasus* [Online] [Read 21/06/2019] Available at:
http://www.iranicaonline.org/articles/clothing-vii

As stated above, the disparity of wealth between the regular people and the aristocracy wasn't as accentuated as in the Scythian society, or at least when it comes to the burial mounds, and so, historians assume that very few individuals would obtain more wealth than the others and that it wasn't so much as to leave a large wealth gap. However, this is true only for the few centuries of their presence in the Black Sea area because as they became successful by the fourth to the first century BCE, wealth came pouring in, and only those with the most power would gain the more significant share. This wealth disparity would increase over time, as each figurehead would break tribal communal traditions and accumulate wealth for themselves.[55]

Sarmatian societal roles placed women in a place of great influence, similar to the Scythians. Not only did women participate in some form of the priesthood and hold religious importance, but they would also fight alongside men on the battlefield. A large number of burial mounds with graves of women warriors have been found, attesting to the equal role of women and men in warfare. Some burial mounds have been found where women were buried in a central position and accompanied by many riches, so we know that Sarmatian women could hold positions of societal importance and had the power to accumulate vast sums of wealth. The Greek tales of the mythical Amazonian warriors originated from the Sarmatian tribes since, according to some classical authors such as Hippocrates and Pomponius Mela, Sarmatian women could only marry after they had faced an enemy on the battlefield.[56]

The account of the classical writer Pomponius Mela goes as follows:

> They are warlike, free, unconquered, and so savage and cruel that women also go to war side by side with men; and so that women may be suited for action, their right breast is cauterized as soon as they are born. As a result, that breast,

---

[55] Sinor, Denis – *The Cambridge History of Early....* p. 116
[56] Sinor, Denis – *The Cambridge History of Early....* p. 111 & 112. Brzezinski, R; Mielczarek, M – *The Sarmatians*. p. 43

now exposed and ready to withstand blows, develops like a man's chest. Archery, horseback riding, and hunting are a girl's pursuits; to kill the enemy is a woman's military duty, so much so that not to have struck one down is considered a scandal, and virginity is the punishment for those women.[57]

Slavery was a part of Sarmatian society, but evidence points to the fact that the Sarmatians only used slaves domestically or as an object to trade.[58] However, they would maintain certain conquered peoples as serfs who did most of the agricultural work for them. Evidence points to people like the Limigantes, who lived-in modern-day Romania, of having that societal and economic task.

---

[57] Mela, Pomponius – *De Situ Orbis*. Transl. F.E. Romer. Michigan: University of Michigan.1998 p.110

[58] Sinor, Denis – *The Cambridge History of Early...*. p. 116

Chapter 9 – Warfare and Conquest

Warfare and conflict were an essential part of the Sarmatian society, and their culture, economy, and society were built around warfare, pillaging, and conquering. From hunting to looting, the Sarmatians knew that to survive in the steppes, one had to be not only mobile but bold and strong. From the fourth century BCE onward, their fame as formidable and ruthless warriors grew, and soon enough, they would be hired as mercenaries by the Pontic and Bosporan Kingdoms and later the Romans.

The first written account of the Sauromatae in the classical sources is about their participation with the Scythian force against the Persian king Darius I in 513 BCE. It's no mere coincidence that when the classical authors mentioned them later in their texts that it had to do mostly with their conflicts and the way they fought. The extent of their collaboration is not entirely known, but Herodotus mentions them as allies of the Scythians.[59]

The Sarmatian tribes had many military encounters throughout their written history. The Aorsi fought on the Roman side in the Roman-Bosporan War in 49 CE, and the Siraces fought on the opposite side. This Bosporan conflict was created when the Bosporan king

---

[59] Brzezinski, R; Mielczarek, M – *The Sarmatians.* p. 7

Aspurgus died and left the kingdom to his son, Mithridates III. The claim of Mithridates was strengthened when the Roman emperor Claudius made him ruler of all the Bosporan territories, although they remained as a client-state of the Romans. However, in 45 CE, for reasons we don't fully understand, Claudius deposed Mithridates and placed Cotys I, Mithridates' younger brother, on the throne. To protect his new client-king emperor, Claudius placed Gaius Julius Aquila in charge of a few Roman cohorts.

Mithridates couldn't stand idly by and watch his treasonous brother claim the throne that he felt was his, so he sought help from a neighboring Sarmatian tribe, the Siraces, who was under King Zorsines. Cotys feared an impending invasion and turned to Gaius Julius Aquila and his cohorts for help. Gaius was a shrewd general, and seeing that Mithridates' forces were much larger in number than theirs, he quickly enlisted the help of another Sarmatian tribe, the Aorsi, who was under King Eunones. As soon as their forces were prepared, Eunones and Aquila attacked the opposing side. The Roman forces began to lay siege to the Bosporan cities under Mithridates' control, such as Artezian, while the Aorsi invaded the Siracen territories and laid siege to the settlement of Uspe. This Siracen city had weak defenses, which enabled the Aorsi to construct tall towers which they could use to harass the defenders with arrows and darts. Uspe's defense was unsustainable and quickly fell to Aorsi control. The siege would only last one day, according to the Roman historian Tiberius, and it would result in the surrender of the Siraces.

When Mithridates received word of his ally's surrender and seeing that his forces were dwindling, he decided to surrender personally to King Eunones, since he knew that the Romans and his brother would kill him. Tiberius describes that Mithridates went to Eunones' court and kneeled before him, saying, "Mithridates, whom the Romans have sought so many years by land and sea, stands before you by his own choice. Deal as you please with the descendant of the great Achaemenes, the only glory of which enemies have not robbed me."

The Sarmatian king was impressed by his courage and, considering that the Aorsi was the only tribe capable of protecting him against Roman aggression, allowed Mithridates to take refuge in the Sarmatian court. However, Eunones could not put his alliance with the Romans at risk to protect a deposed prince and wrote to the Roman emperor informing him of Mithridates' presence in his court but also asked that he show mercy to the deposed Bosporan king. Claudius showed his mercy but ordered Mithridates to be sent to Rome. After an audience with the emperor, Mithridates was let go and forgiven.[60]

The Aorsi-Roman force secured a victory for their coalition and brought such devastation to the Siraces that they would only appear once more in the classic books as a co-belligerent in the Bosporan conflict of 193 CE. After that, they vanish from written history. Although the Aorsi chose the winning side in the Bosporan War in 49 CE, some decades later, they would be conquered and assimilated by the powerful Alans who had recently arrived in the Black Sea area.[61]

The Iazyges and Roxolani, who had crossed the Don in the second century BCE, were in an advantageous position in the first century BCE, having close proximity to the Roman border and thus access to direct diplomatic relations with the Roman Empire as well as the possibility to loot some of their wealthier cities. For the duration of the first century CE, the Iazyges were relatively friendly with the Romans and helped them in their military agendas. However, the Roxolani conducted a series of raids on Roman Moesia from 62 to 86 CE, even managing to destroy a Roman legion. This destruction reminded the Roman generals that the Sarmatian peoples were a serious foe, and even their superior army structure couldn't compete with the large numbers of cavalrymen the Sarmatians had in their hosts.

---

[60] Tacitus – *The Annals*. Book XII. [Online] [Read 20/06/2019] Available at: http://classics.mit.edu/Tacitus/annals.8.xii.html
[61] Brzezinski, R; Mielczarek, M – *The Sarmatians*. p. 8

The Roxolani also participated in the Dacian Wars, siding with the Dacian peoples against the Roman invaders. In this war, the Romans enlisted the help of the Iazyges who had been receptive toward them previously. At the end of the Dacian Wars, Roman emperor Trajan won the conflict against the Dacian-Roxolani combined force and managed to antagonize both Sarmatian tribes (Roxolani and Iazyges) by establishing and demarcating the imperial province of Dacia, infringing on Sarmatian control in the area. They would engage in many conflicts with the Roman Empire after this, only being temporarily pacified when Roman Emperor Hadrian allowed them to coexist in Roman-controlled Dacia. In this pacification process, the Roxolani king, Rasparagnus, was given Roman citizenship, and subsidies were paid to the Roxolani to maintain some stability with the borders. The Marcomannic Wars (166–180 CE) during the reign of Roman Emperor Marcus Aurelius marked a reopening of their hostilities with the Sarmatians as the Iazyges joined with Germanic forces to invade the Roman provinces of Pannonia and Dacia. Marcus Aurelius ultimately defeated them, and peace was made. The truce between the two would be finalized by the handing over of 8,000 Sarmatian horsemen. For this victory, Marcus Aurelius would adopt the title of "Sarmaticus," a title that openly displayed to the Romans that Aurelius was the one to subdue and achieve great victories against the Sarmatians.[62]

The first Alanic military conflict that is mentioned in classical literature is the Alanic incursion into Parthia in 73 CE. What essentially was a looting military incursion by the Alans resulted in the death of Armenian King Tiridates in battle, who was trying to defend his homeland from Sarmatian sacking.

In 135 CE, another account of an Alanic looting incursion is mentioned, this time into Asia Minor via the Caucasus Mountains. This endeavor was eventually driven back by Arrian, the Roman governor of the province of Cappadocia, a region in modern-day Turkey. The beginning of the second century CE would mark the

---

[62] Brzezinski, R; Mielczarek, M – *The Sarmatians*. p. 9

Alanic arrival in the Black Sea area where they assimilated and conquered the local Sarmatians such as the Aorsi.[63]

The military organization of the Sarmatian units from the seventh to the fourth century BCE was of tribal origin and would require all men and women who could fight to report to the battlefield where individuals of power would command their small local groups. These individuals would then answer to the commands of the tribal king or chief. From the fourth century onward, the Sarmatians developed a social structure around warfare, and warriors would only be the ones explicitly chosen to fight on the battlefield, whether they were men or women, not just all able-bodied individuals. A warrior "caste" thus arose.[64] The Greek author Lucian gives us an idea of how the hordes of Sarmatian warriors were raised:

> Our custom of the hide is as follows. When a man has been injured by another, and desires vengeance, but feels that he is no match for his opponent, he sacrifices an ox, cuts up the flesh and cooks it, and spreads out the hide upon the ground. On this hide, he takes his seat, holding his hands behind him, so as to suggest that his arms are tied in that position, this being the natural attitude of a suppliant among us. Meanwhile, the flesh of the ox has been laid out; and the man's relations and any others who feel so disposed come up and take a portion thereof, and, setting their right foot on the hide, promise whatever assistance is in their power: one will engage to furnish and maintain five horsemen, another ten, a third some larger number; while others, according to their ability, promise heavy or light-armed infantry, and the poorest, who have nothing else to give, offer their own personal services. The number of persons assembled on the hide is sometimes very considerable; nor could any troops be more reliable or more invincible than those which are collected in this manner, being as they are under a vow; for

---

[63] Brzezinski, R; Mielczarek, M – *The Sarmatians*. p. 10
[64] Brzezinski, R; Mielczarek, M – *The Sarmatians*. p. 14

the act of stepping on to the hide constitutes an oath. By this means, then, Arsacomas raised something like 5,000 cavalry and 20,000 heavy and light-armed.[65]

Although one could say that the Sarmatians dedicated themselves professionally to warfare, considering their civilization and culture depended on it, they didn't have a professional army structure like the Roman Empire did. The Sarmatian method of raising an army was similar to those of the Celts or the Gauls where individuals pled their loyalty to one man or cause, who in turn promised them booty and plunder. However, this is only true of their military organization until the second century CE, since Sarmatian society became more hierarchical from the second to the fourth century CE, and warriors were chosen and trained according to their skills. As such, between those centuries, a special kind of Sarmatian cavalry unit, the armored lancer, was formed to help support the Sarmatian armies with the use of the long lance.[66]

The cavalry was at the core of the Sarmatian army, and the most common unit of the cavalry was the light-armored horse archer; they would be accompanied by better-armored lancers who constituted the minority of the forces. Some historical records state that they used infantry, but it is likely that either it was constituted mainly of non-Sarmatian peoples (i.e., assimilated peoples) or of poorer Sarmatians who could not afford to own a horse.[67] The Alans, for instance, had an aversion of being on foot and considered it beneath them, which is confirmed by Ammianus Marcellinus who states, "Therefore, all those who through age or sex are unfit for war to remain close by the wagons and are occupied in light tasks; but the

---

[65] The Works of Lucian of Samosata. Translated by Fowler, H W and F G. Oxford: The Clarendon Press. 1905. [Online] [29/05/2019]. Available at: https://lucianofsamosata.info/Toxaris.html. Entry 48.
[66] Brzezinski, R; Mielczarek, M – *The Sarmatians*. p. 15
[67] Brzezinski, R; Mielczarek, M – *The Sarmatians*. p. 19 & 20

young men grow up in the habit of riding from their earliest boyhood and regard it as contemptible to go on foot..."[68]

The armor the Sarmatian soldiers used was made of mostly leather, hide, or iron. Bronze armor would be used by only the richest warriors since it was expensive and difficult to make. The famous scale armor of iron and bronze, a characteristic that they also shared with the Scythians, has been found in archaeological findings amongst the Sauromatae of the sixth century BCE. However, only the wealthiest of warriors would be able to afford it. The less wealthy would sew individual scales to their hide or leather armor. A different type of armor, the mail, has only been found in archaeological findings of the first century CE. The Sarmatians first used mail armor to complement the use of scale armor in the torso area, which was less technologically advanced, and would also use mail armor to cover their arms and legs. Only in the second century CE do we find complete sets of mail armor being used by the Sarmatians. Around this century, another type of scale armor also appeared one that was less resource-demanding and made from local materials like horns or horse hooves that were then enclosed in the scale form. [69]

The helmets of the Sarmatian aristocracy, like their armor, would be made of metal, and the earliest of these was the Greek Corinthian helmets that were modified to not restrict the vision of the wearer as much. From the second century CE to the fourth CE, around the Black Sea area, another Greek helmet would replace the Corinthian, the Greek pileus, as well as other Celtic and Italo-Etruscan varieties. The Greek pileus was a very basic helmet, essentially consisting of a cone-shaped metal hat that only protected the individual's cranium. At the end of the first century CE, one peculiar helmet gained considerable popularity. It was made of curved iron plates that were placed beneath an iron skeleton made of three or four vertical bands

---

[68] Marcellinus, Ammianus – *Rerum Gestarum*. Book 31. 2.20 [Online] [Read 30/05/2019] Available at: http://penelope.uchicago.edu/Thayer/E/Roman/Texts/Ammian/home.html
[69] Brzezinski, R; Mielczarek, M – *The Sarmatians*. p. 20 & 21

and riveted to two horizontal hoops; it is often portrayed as the precursor of the medieval Spangenhelm.[70]

The Sarmatians used three main weapons: the spear/lance, the sword, and the bow. The spear and long lance would be used on horseback and would allow the user to kill their enemy at a safe distance, especially with the case of the long lance. The Iranian *acinaces*, also spelled *akinakes*, was a short sword (50-60 centimeters, or a little over 1.5 feet) they used, although there were swords that were longer (around 70 centimeters, or a little over 2 feet). The latter would be especially useful for horseback combat since that required long-range weapons. The primitive bow of the early Sarmatian period would consist of various pieces of wood glued together and was usually no longer than 80 centimeters (a little over 2.5 feet) in length. It was only from the first century CE onward that the Sarmatians adopted the so-called Hunnic bow that was larger, measuring 120 centimeters (almost 4 feet) in length, and was made of much stronger composite materials.[71]

---

[70] Brzezinski, R; Mielczarek, M – *The Sarmatians.* p. 22
[71] Brzezinski, R; Mielczarek, M – *The Sarmatians.* p. 24-34

Chapter 10 – End of the Sarmatians

The Sarmatian period ends in a very similar way as the Scythian one did, with the vast migration of the Goths from Scandinavia and Central Asia. They swept the Black Sea area westward and either destroyed entire tribes or integrated tribes who they conquered on their way. Let's take a look at how each Sarmatian tribe ended their period of glory around the Black Sea region.

As mentioned before, the Sauromatae ended with the arrival and conquest/assimilation of them by the Siraces and Aorsi in the 5th to 4th century BCE; the Siraces vanished after the Bosporan conflict of 193 CE, perhaps assimilated by the Aorsi; and the Aorsi would end with the arrival of the Alans in the Black Sea area in the mid-first century CE, being conquered/assimilated by them.

The Iazyges and Roxolani, who had crossed the Don well before the Alans arrived, survived some conflicts with the Roman Empire but were ultimately assimilated into the empire between the third and fourth centuries CE, who then used their territories as a natural barrier against the hordes of Gothic invaders. This act established Dacia and Pannonia as the land of the Danubian Sarmatians, where they maintained some degree of cultural identity and autonomy but were regarded as part of the Roman Empire.[72]

Lastly, the Alans were driven out of their position of dominance over the northern Black Sea area when the Gothic peoples arrived in the first half of the third century. This moment marked the beginning of a process that scattered the various Alanic tribes which constituted the Alanic federation decades before the invasions of the Goths. By the time of the Gothic invasions or migration to the Black Sea area, the first split occurred, and some Alans stayed with the Gothic peoples and were assimilated by them while the larger group of Alans retreated to the east of the Don.

The Goths, who since the first century CE had been migrating in waves from their ancestral lands in Scandinavia to Central and Eastern Europe, were, in the fourth century, divided amongst two major groups: the Visigoths and the Ostrogoths. The Visigoths, who were Roman *foederati* (similar to vassals), occupied the area of the Danube River, while the Ostrogoths, who had much more contact with the Huns, occupied the northern Black Sea coast. These peoples had already assimilated the majority of the Sarmatian communities that lived in the Black Sea area, either politically, in the sense that some tribes were under the rule of the Gothic kings, or demographically, where they integrated most of the ethnic Sarmatians into their own cultural group.

The part of the Alans who managed to escape west at the time of the Hunnic arrival into the Black Sea area would be found with all types of tribes, including the Goths and other Germanic tribes. In 378, we know that a group of Alans participated in the Battle of Adrianople on the side of the Visigothic revolt against the Romans. This battle resulted in a victory for the Visigoths thanks to the swift action of the Alanic cavalry, which not only intercepted the Roman cavalry but also flanked the Roman infantry, allowing the Visigothic infantry to engage more easily with the Roman battle line. This Gothic and

---

[72] Brzezinski, R; Mielczarek, M – *The Sarmatians.* p. 7 & 8.

Alanic victory would start the beginning of the end of the hegemony of the Roman Empire in Europe, as the defeat of Adrianople was, at the time, the worst Roman defeat since the Battle of Edessa against the Persian Sassanids in 260 CE.

The last semi-autonomous Alanic group we have a record of is the one that crossed the Rhine with the Germanic Vandals and Suebi and managed to reach Spain and North Africa, at which point they were assimilated by the Vandals. In 416, the Vandal king would continue to use the title of "Rex Vandalorum et Alanorum" as a way of demonstrating his control over the Alanic peoples that still lived with the Vandals.

In the fourth century CE, a nomadic confederation of nomadic Turkic people, the Huns, was coming from the east into the Black Sea area, and they were much more numerous than any Sarmatian and Gothic tribal confederation that lived there. They apparently operated with vicious cruelty and were formidable mounted warriors that relied on their powerful horse archers to inflict heavy casualties to infantry forces before they could engage them. The threat the Huns posed to the Goths made them migrate into the Roman Empire together with some of the Alans. However, other Alanic tribes managed to coexist to an extent with the Hunnic peoples. This, however, wouldn't last for long, and in the late fourth century CE, the remaining Alans that still lived in the Black Sea region were conquered by the Huns, either being killed or assimilated. Unfortunately, we don't have any type of information on how the battles between the Alans and the Huns were conducted or where they took place. The Alans under Hunnic rule would accompany them in their ravaging of the Roman Empire in the 5th century CE under the rule of Attila the Hun. Eventually, the Alans became so assimilated into the Huns that classical historians could no longer make a distinction between the two. The ones who managed to survive went with the Goths, traveled farther west to merge with the Vandals and Suebi, or were integrated into the Roman Empire. The arrival of the Huns in the fourth century CE permanently marked the end of the Alans as a confederation and as a social unit. Only one of the scattered Alanic tribes managed to survive the Hunnic invasion and maintain some semblance of cultural identity, who were those that fled south to the Caucasus Mountains and managed to survive to the modern day in the form of the Ossetians.[73]

The demise of the Alans marked the end of Indo-Iranian domination of the northern Black Sea, but the remains of their presence would be preserved through historical artifacts and writings from primary sources. Today, we cannot only admire their material culture and artistic output in museums and expositions, but we can also continue to write about their history so that they may never be entirely lost to time again.

---

[73] Brzezinski, R; Mielczarek, M – *The Sarmatians*. p. 24-34. Sinor, Denis – *The Cambridge History of Early...*. p. 112

Conclusion

The Indo-Iranian peoples of the Scythian and Sarmatian tribes shared more similarities throughout their existence than many people think. Not only did they share the same language, but they also shared the same nomadic or semi-nomadic way of life, a similar art style, the related culture of warfare and horseback riding, the high placement of women in their societal hierarchy, similar economic structures, and much more. Although they were different people, more things brought them together than placed them apart.

Even though they are no longer around as a unified cultural group, their legacy as ruthless warriors and nomadic herders lives on to this day, thanks to the writers of antiquity who, good or bad, wrote about their way of life. In a way, they never ceased to exist.

The Scythians and Sarmatians, due to not having a written record and being mostly lost through time as they were assimilated by conquering peoples, don't have the popularity amongst the general public that they should have, especially Western audiences. Many academic works have been written in Russian, Romanian, and Polish, among others, but the English translation of these works is very sparse, which means that researching this topic is particularly tricky to non-Eastern Europeans. Perhaps the lack of interest among the international public, outside of a few cases, keeps the academic papers and books about these Indo-Iranian peoples from being published, even though the literary world would only be enriched by these translations.

Here's another book by Captivating History you might be interested in

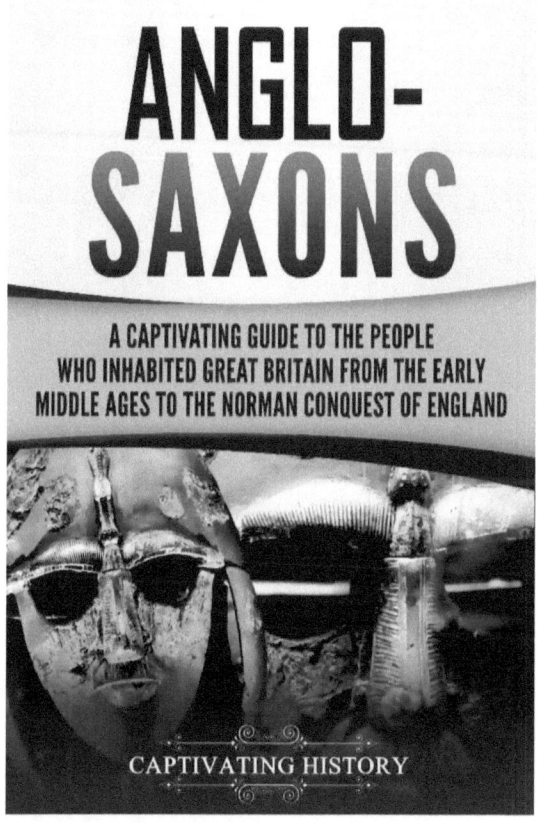

www.ingramcontent.com/pod-product-compliance
Lightning Source LLC
LaVergne TN
LVHW090039080526
838202LV00046B/3873